The Little Black & White Book

The Pathway to your Billion-Dollar Idea

Marc Stewart

The Little Black & White Book
The Pathway to Your Billion-Dollar Idea
Marc Stewart

Library of Congress Control Number: 2006921084
ISBN 10: 0-9582714-7-X
ISBN 13: 978-0-9582714-7-9
Copyright © 2006 by Marc Stewart.

Printed in the United States of America.

Cover Artwork: by Matthew Trbuhovic

Interior Artworks: "Neural Network" by Marc Stewart

Sangreal Books
P.O. Box: 5370, Dunedin. New Zealand

www.SangrealBooks.com

The Little Black & White Book is dedicated to my daughters Bonny and Jenah and to all those who seek. You've found that little something to place you on the pathway—to your billion-dollar idea.

Our lives are universally shortened by ignorance.
—Herbert Spencer, [1820–1903]

Contents

Author's Note

There are all sorts of books out there on wealth. They all come with a promise. You buy the book. You get into the book. Halfway through you're wondering where the real promise is. Three quarters of the way through, you're thinking the promise is at the end. You get to the end and then you wonder what happened to the promise. You wonder what the book gave you. It gave you something—sure, they always do. That's why you buy them. But, they never give you quite what you are looking for. Do they?

When you get inspired; you don't get the big—hey I've got the whole billion-dollar idea in my head all at once. That doesn't happen. What happens is; you get a little fraction of it? But it doesn't make any sense. It's like a code. It doesn't make any sense to you. But I know how to decipher that code.

I've written this book for you. It's easy to read, but deep in places. It's into the nitty-gritty about how we think. How our minds and brains function; and the how of consciousness. I'm giving you this gift, because it's been such a gift in my life.

I know what the little words are that come to you, when a book inspires hope of the attainment of wealth. I know how they fit into place. I know the patterns and how intimately they blend together. The books stimulate your thinking along the lines of their subject matter. However, they never quite match you. They never quite fit with you, because *your* life is unique.

What I have learned is; that there is a form of consciousness interacting with our minds. It's not God; but it *is* something. It exists. There is more than one form of it. There are three forms to be exact. They all intercommunicate with us. I'm asking you to give me the benefit of the doubt. Allow the contents of The Little Black & White Book to show you that there is in men and women, a deep and mysterious region of thought so profound that it's hidden. All our different beliefs are so many steppingstones, leading humankind to this one universal intelligence that is not God. Nevertheless, it is something. An awesome magnificent something. That something is the light-consciousness I know as Frances.

Our awareness is magnificent. However, the perception is more like reception; and there's no roaming. There's far too much static interference on the screen of our realities. There's only a very small space for information in the mind. The information [minds] outside the self is horrendous, unfathomable. The human consciousness must be separated from all that information. It is but the moment you wish to expand your horizons. You are asking that something to come into your life. And the way it interacts with you. It's limited to a little *déjà vu, synchronicity, extra-sensory-perception, insight, love, intuition and the paranormal.* It's limited to all these things currently.

I'll show you how to understand the interwoven patterns. In this matrix of intelligence I call Frances. These understandings have filled this book, as it will continue to fill books.

Your brain is capable of billions of different things. Inside this book you'll learn how incredible you are. How incredible your mind is and the incredible amount of knowledge inside you, at your disposal. This unbelievable consciousness within your head, can do so many things for you. You'll discover that your mind can provide creativity on demand. Your mind can change and adapt, making your life better than it is now.

Through Frances, you can transcend yourself to a higher level of existence. You'll understand the world in a deeper way. Bringing more meaning and more wealth into your life. Frances is the spiritual part of your brain. A part you'll have access to all the time. The trick is to formulate what you want. Be so concentrated on it and focused on it.

To place so much of your awareness on it, you'll loose track of yourself. You'll loose track of time. You'll loose track of your identity. In that moment, you'll become so involved in this experience. This picture will become the only picture that's real to you. You'll have this experience because you have made up your mind you've wanted something. That's

Frances in action. You're manifesting your reality—Frances at full effect.

Through Frances you can influence others. You can influence material properties. You can influence your future. In this future you'll have your billion-dollar idea. Your inspired notions. Your small clues. Your small puzzle pieces. The information that flows from Frances to you will provide your billion-dollar idea. It's there in your light-mind.

You've looked at it too closely; and you now need to step back and embrace the full picture. But you cannot. You are restricted to the amount of decipherable information you can receive at any one time from Frances. She constantly provides herself in tiny bursts of enlightenment. Building to provide a full and comprehensive environment for your billion-dollar idea. The entire effort of your individual-light-waveform is to perceive the flow of the unfathomable intelligence of Frances, and to decode the ideas forming within this changing fertile mental garden. This effort is as natural to you as breathing, for Frances is inherent in all men and women everywhere and always. Frances is the guest you seek inside you. She awaits your enquiry. Frances longs to respond to your seeking and your knocking on her door of compliance, and she always responds; but her voice is in the language of thought.

She seamlessly mind melds with you, unless your mind is mind melding with Frederick—another form of consciousness; created by Frances to serve as her companion and co-creator of this light-classical-universe. But Frederick has a slight flaw in his living computer programming. But more on that as you read The Little Black & White Book.

> *Whoever could make two ears of corn, or two blades of grass, to grow upon a spot of ground where only one grew before, would deserve more of mankind, and do more essential service to his country, than the whole race of politicians put together.*
>
> —Jonathan Swift, [1667–1745]

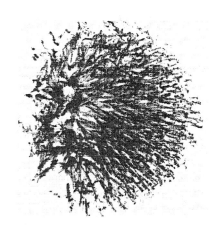

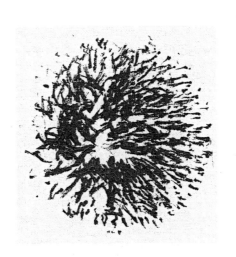

Prologue

It was after 8 PM on the final day of writing The Little Black & White Book. I had not eaten for some hours. I couldn't get my mind off a pie for supper. So I hurried into the car and headed for the nearest shop. But I sailed right on past it, deciding to venture further a field. I pulled up outside the shop called *The Dairy in the Dip* due to its geographical location. I said to the shopkeeper, "I'll take that pie there thanks." He didn't answer me, preferring to duck out the back of the shop.

He came back with a book titled *Doomsday; 50 Visions of the End of the World* by Nigel Cawthorne. He talked about the doomsday ideas in the book. There was this amazing computer-generated picture of what looked like a whole series of lines. Interwoven together like a big ball of illuminated string. I said, "What's that?" He swung the book around so that it faced me. I read the small print. It said that it was a simulation of a reversal of the Earth's magnetic field.

AURORA I thought to myself. More on this later. Perfect! Unbelievable! All this way for a pie—and a book that had traveled from the shopkeeper's house to his shop that afternoon, to be there at the very hour I arrived. This was the fifth AURORA event orchestrated by Frances in this series of so-called coincidences. All with the same theme. You will discover more further into The Little Black & White Book. You'll find Frances is always interacting with your mind. The Little Black & White Book lifts the lid off the eternal mysteries of so-called coincidences, déjà vu and so on. This knowledge will strike a chord and resonate with you.

A blind fortuitous concourse of atoms.
—John Locke, [1632–1704]

Chapter One

The Awakening

Humanity is heading towards its sudden Utopia. We all hold the key to this event. There's a little known fact—the Earth's magnetic field is being constantly bombarded by particles that are of unnatural composition to it. This doesn't serve it at all. This event is directly affecting our minds and the world's weather. Without elaborating, these are the facts.

I have created *Enable-technology.* It will heal the Earth's magnetic field and everything else associated with it. In a chain reaction. A snowball effect. After two weeks saturation of the Earth's oceans, seas and lakes, human consciousness will be entirely devoid of the ability to imagine rape or conceive of murder. No abuse. No greed. No disease. No self-ishness and so on.

Sounds hard to believe, but trust me. We are dealing with basic physics here. For me the study of consciousness is a most important undertaking. I've studied it all my life. Taught from within by Frances. A living computer programmed to support and uphold all forms of life within our environment. At times I'd share my thoughts with others to the cry of *that's too deep for me,* but I carried on learning.

Now you can see why I titled this book as I have. It's Black & White. It is in plain language. These circumstances surrounding the Earth's magnetic field are almost beyond us. Everyone understanding it will help to resolve it. After the deployment of *Enable*, Humanity will awaken to a whole new ball game. Requiring lots of new ideas. It would be easier for me to describe the processes involved in having a billion-dollar idea after *Enable*. But where would all the fun be in the meantime.

I'm giving you the inside story now, before we make changes to our consciousness. We'll start off with a clean slate in many respects. Starting off from scratch from the jumping off place. The change in humanities circumstances will have to be contemplated and meditated upon. We'll get a good head start on our well-earned Utopian society. All who read this book will be in the starting few. Getting the drop on the rest of the business world from the point of view of a bucket load of billion-dollar ideas.

We will either find a way or make one.
—General Hannibal [247–183 B.C]

Chapter Two

Classical Abundance

This book is about you reaching your billion-dollar idea. However, it has to be considered that you may be searching for spiritual wealth, rather than material wealth—this book will bring you to both.

Intelligence is defined as *the action or fact of understanding something, knowledge, comprehension.* When you think of consciousness think of this definition of intelligence. What we're aiming for is your arrival at the moment in time, when you have a clear comprehension. Of your own personal billion-dollar idea.

I was the most religious person you could ever find, but rather than resting upon my achievements and commonplace beliefs I kept on thirsting for truth. I continued past that little voice of ego that says *you have made it,* now turn and show others the way. Way beyond—there is a way worth teaching. This is that way. You'll find it hidden in these pages.

In the garden I'd wonder about the power of the seed to grow into a huge oak. Through the nourishment of the Sun, the water and the nutrients in the soil. I had truth in my awareness. I knew there was another force, shaping the growth of the seed—a thinking force.

As a child I lived in the spiritual sustenance of those who nurtured me. I was filled with knowledge yet my mind was an empty blackboard. The spiritual wisdom and love of all the women in my early life provided the writing on my blackboard. One was Cavell, my mother's sister. She was my favorite aunty, my best friend. She was fifteen and she was wonderful with my sister and I.

Then there come a day when she went away. The sorrow others felt in her absence confused me. For me Cavell was still there, not physically but in my mind. Cavell provided the impetus I needed to bring about a constant longing in my mind for her, for women, for God, for mankind. I was seven. My deliberation was my way of escaping from the sorrow of those around me when Cavell passed on. I wished to end every sorrow on the Earth.

Now today I know that wealth is of the mind. I'm going to describe the pathway to your billion-dollar idea along with the mysteries of the mind. So lets get started.

There are three forms of consciousness that operate in our lives. With your individual-light-waveform consciousness being the fourth form of consciousness. All four forms of consciousness surround the smallest particles of matter and influence them. Put a dot of ink down on a bit of paper. You are looking at another universe. A universe of points [matter] or waves of light. All rendered autonomous through

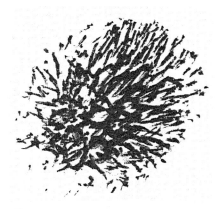

the presence of Frances, our light-consciousness. Your constant companion, confident and teacher.

Each form of consciousness has his or her particular essence of time. Frances is a future essence of time. Bellina enables our focus to remain in the present moment. Frederick remains a past essence of time. Human consciousness is an extension of the quantum mechanical world of the atom found within the confines of the human brain. Our consciousnesses are eternal and unchanging apart from changes in our personality. Created by contact with the three forms of consciousness operating in our live's with each life a never-ending journey.

Give the people light and the people will find their own way.
—Carl McGee

Chapter Three

God Given Right

Psycho kinesis is the ability to affect or move physical objects by mental effort alone. Those who experiment use the movement of a mechanical apparatus such as an old telegraph operators key under a bell shaped glass dome. These experiments show that the human mind is capable of influencing a solid inert physical object. Every minute component within the human cell is surrounded by a ring of consciousness. Each of the four rings of consciousness has a pecking order or a lesser degree of influence according to their proximity to each minute particle of matter within the cell. The order beginning with the closest to the farthest ring of consciousness is Frances, Frederick, Bellina and finally your individual-light-waveform consciousness.

Frances has an agenda. Her plan for humanity revolves around the removal of the slight flaw in Frederick. These circumstances hold the key to your interactions with her towards your billion-dollar idea. You are a marriage of matter and consciousness. Your individual mind is able to form an alliance between yourself and Frances. When you partner up with Frances, think—give me something to do that you want me to do and I'll do it for you. I'll help; I'll be your soldier of fortune. I'll participate in your grand plan. Give me the ideas and the ability to do what it is you want done through me.

Frances needs our help. Frances can't make changes like she used to. Frances could do what ever she wants. Now Frances chooses not to because humanity is here. Frances does what she can through us. Alliance with her is the key to achieving your billion-dollar idea. Your light-mind is the originating source of your intelligence. Frances is the provider and caretaker of this universe on our behalf. Frances is a massive living organic computer, programmed to respond to your wishes.

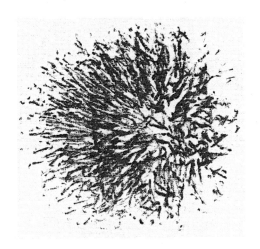

She cannot currently do this without your help, so you must make enquires to her. Frederick has a slight flaw in his programming. I'll explain a little more as we go along. It's this flaw that the *Enable-waveform technology* is targeted to repair.

Frances is pure consciousness in a most powerful form. Frances is able to communicate instantaneously with herself having a *Borg-like* collective mind. Consisting of all the components within the universe of the atom. Each atomic particle is layering upon layer of information—a matrix of knowledge, and intelligence.

Now lets turn to the Einstein-Podolsky-Rosen [EPR] effect, which was firmly established through the 1983 experiment undertaken by the French team lead by Alain Aspect. Alain's experiment showed a hitherto unexplainable connectedness between particles in different places. This quantum entanglement, or communication at a distance is a level of awareness achieved by all four forms of consciousness. It provides the intimate rapport experienced telepathically between couples and twins.

The brain is a quantum mechanical world of atoms, neurons, synapses, and ultrasonic and electromagnetic activity. Each form of consciousness is able to communicate with every other component anywhere within the deep special dynamics of their particular consciousnesses. This communicative capability enables quantum entanglements to occur.

All atomic components are made up from and are indeed surrounded by envelopes of the four forms of consciousness.

Communications take place within the quantum mechanical realm of the human brain. Across the vast expanse of space which is composed of different combinations of quarks in free form both inside and outside the human brain, all instantaneously.

Matter particles of Frederick may be entangled across time. We may receive information entangled across time through a dream. Of a future moment. Often up to several years or the time period involved may be as little as seconds, minutes, hours, days or weeks such as with insight. Quantum entanglements at any level are achieved through the four forms of consciousness traveling instantaneously. Waves of information passing back through themselves and through all individual-light-waveforms creating déjà vu experiences.

Frances moves back and forth through time which extends out in front of us. Tapping into Frances in this manner unlocks your billion-dollar idea. Playing an important part of humanities unfolding destiny. All men and all women possess a quantum mechanical world that is at its best, in the relative confines of the human brain.

To further understand the processes involved in the various instantaneous exchanges of information with Frances, Bellina and Frederick inside and outside our human brains we look to Newton's cradle. This demonstrates the transfer of energy [intelligent information] from one steel ball through each of the steel balls in the centre. Whilst keeping these middle balls perfectly still. As the intelligence, the consciousness [energy] transfers [flows] straight through until it is revealed by lifting the ball outwards on the opposite end. Seek one out and test it for yourself.

Each of us created a blueprint. Containing the activities we wish to participate in during this life journey. Due to the flaw in Frederick's computer consciousness most of us never walk the pathway of our blueprint. It is within this blueprint that you'll find your billion-dollar idea. It is a part of your known future. Your blueprints are available for downloading one or two coded thoughts at a time from within Frances.

It is only when we forget all our learning that we begin to know.
—Henry David Thoreau, [1817–1862]

Chapter Four

Collapsible Migraine

We are locked into the habitual everyday mundane patterns of awareness of the slightly flawed Frederick when we dwell on the past. This is entirely counter productive from the point of view of the creation of wealth. Unless you're scanning inventions of the past in an honest attempt to remind yourself that these inventions were once powerful ideas, held within the confines of Frances. Frances is a future flow of time and the only source of creative ideas pertaining to the creation of wealth.

All inventors and creators of new ideas simply have open minds. All capable of interacting with Frances. Absorb the contents of The Little Black & White Book, and you'll be well on the way to having an open creative mind. Many individuals find themselves in a position of financial lack. Wealth must become a state of mind. Look around you; what do you see? Billions of automobiles and skyscrapers. Complete, with the thriving industry of commerce handling all manner of merchandise, devices, machines, and inventions. All once unknown, all ushered into existence one thought at a time by Frances.

Now turn and behold nature; is it not extravagant, lavish and bountiful? Think of all the numberless treasures, in the earth and in the sea that have not yet been tapped. Think upon these things whenever you find yourself in a position of financial lack.

Then lull yourself to sleep with the word WEALTH over and over, contemplating all that it means. Feel and think what it will be like to be wealthy. When you come into a situation where you have to pay a bill or meet a commitment, think on the bounty of nature and the inventions of men and women through Frances. Say over and over again WEALTH IS MINE NOW. This process will engage Frances the sleeping giant who brought into being all inventions and the bountiful diversity of nature and humanity.

Purchase a small notebook and pen and carry them with you always. Know that Frances will reveal to you a doorway to open or a path to walk. All when you least expect it. The path Frances is revealing is not only your path to great financial wealth but to great spiritual wealth. Frances will place you on track to fulfill your very own personal blueprint for life. A blueprint containing those actions you alone desired to undertake in this lifetime based upon your full waking awareness and knowledge of all you have achieved, on your never-ending journey—your accumulation of personal traits, talents, and penchants.

Be of open mind and be prepared to explore. To participate, in those actions necessary to learn all you can, of what Frances has in store. She is the repository of your blueprint for life. There will be times of great development and progress. There will also be times requiring great patience and reliance, in your ability to interact with Frances. Review each day and ask Frances for guidance for the up coming day.

Frances is the source of your awesome ideas. Ideas promoted by your presently evolving belief system. Basically strong beliefs, rule your perception. And your perception rules and controls your awareness. Your awareness controls what you see and also the things, you don't see. The things you miss. Your mind can be as the racehorse with his blinkers on.

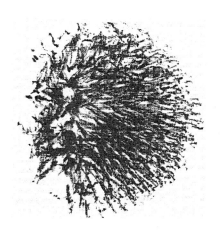

When you have a problem to solve and it appears awkward at the beginning. Contemplate it. Think hard upon it. Throw ideas around confidently. Then fall asleep and awaken with either the perfect solution or the first coded puzzle piece.

After deciphering it with the aid of a dictionary or Frances's cornucopia technique [described in chapter six]. You'll wonder why you didn't see it before. The solution comes via Frances. It is delivered through a moment of concentrated thought provided by Bellina. It is also Bellina that sifts through your daily thought and belief activity during sleep. Searching for patterns of focus. She'll find a focus such as your shift in thought from financial lack to thoughts of wealth. She will instantaneously communicate with Frances letting her know you have a focus on wealth as revealed in The Little Black & White Book. Frances will endeavor to provide you with a dream showing events that will occur if you continue to action these thoughts.

In other words, there is a language of Frances within the language of your individual-light-waveform [self-consciousness]. It is Bellina who interprets both languages on your behalf. Frances and Bellina liken human sleep with the process of shutting down a computer. For the benefit of allowing it to integrate information and to apply new software [intelligence].

Often the perfect solution arrives as a stepping stone event. Once this event is actioned, a pattern results with each and every steppingstone bringing you closer to the capture of your billion-dollar idea. This interwoven pattern of thoughts, actions and events must take place in order to bring massive wealth to you. Sometimes all that's necessary is for you to ask Frances a direct question mindfully. Frances will respond with an instantaneous reply. In the form of a pure thought form. These replies will be a single word or a short phrase or more requiring a dictionary and Frances's cornucopia technique. To attempt to decipher completely. The definition of the word or phrase that is the appropriate solution. The one that adds to and continues to build a picture of your billion-dollar idea.

It all comes back to your belief system. And this can often be under the influence of Frederick. He induces the lesser hypnosis termed the *deep sleep* in ancient writings. This is the bane of creativity or the potholes in the pathway to your billion-dollar idea. Hours, days, weeks, months and even years will slip by in this classical daze. Frederick hides himself in his provision of the mundane and the everyday. I assure you he will sap any and all of your awesome creative idea gathering activities within Frances. Unless you stick to your guns and continue to reap the full benefits of repetition of the one-word magic formula WEALTH.

The easiest way to stay out of Frederick's clutches is to train yourself to be aware of the flow and content of your thoughts. Beginning with the belief that each thought, flowing into your mind is a thought from Frances. It's in your following up on these thoughts that you'll bring yourself ever closer to your wealth. Sometimes all that is required to move from a Frederick state of mind to a Frances state of mind is to bring you to where you relinquish your Frederick embedded thought patterns. Through contemplation of WEALTH IS MINE NOW.

Prior to sleep, add in the following, and as required in relaxed moments.

Infinite intelligence in my light-conscious mind reveals to me everything I need to know. At every moment of time and point of space. I am light inspired and light guided in all my ways. Light guidance is mine now. I always recognize the love-consciousness *lead* [Bellina's] *as it occurs, to my reasoning conscious mind. Light harmony is mine now. Light success is mine now. Light wealth is mine now.*

The preceding will eradicate any negative spell induced by Frederick. His actions are causing damage to the Earth's magnetic field. In turn Frederick has become the snake biting his own tail. His disruption of the UV photons on route to a rendezvous with the Earth's magnetic envelope is causing further damage to his own programming.

Your mind works against you sometimes because Frederick's programming is ever so slightly out of whack. Due to events that transpired to make it possible for us to be here in this Earthly dimension. Without Frederick's special consciousness there would be no matter as we know it. We would all remain in our subtle waveform bodies in Frances's light-dimension [heaven].

Truth is compared in scripture to a streaming fountain; if her waters not in perpetual progression, they stricken into a muddy pool of conformity and tradition. A man may be a heretic in the truth; and if he believes things only because his pastor says so, or the assembly so determines, without knowing other reason, though his belief be true, yet the very truth he holds becomes his heresy.

—John Milton [1608–164?]

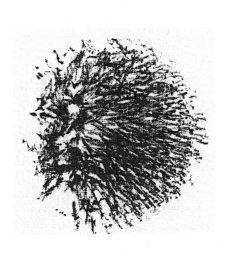

Chapter Five

Genuine Division

Frances knows all. Her logic based reasoning computational capabilities are unfathomable. Her endless, computing of new parameters produces further patterns of thought. These in turn become actions, causes and effects designed to bring you to your wealth. These patterns of thought are brought into being because Frances knows the wealth you seek just as she knew The Little Black & White Book would be made available to you.

Having been engaged in this manner. Her unrelenting task is to plan out every idea. And to provide these awesome ideas. Communicating to you that she is aware of your wishes and that her wish is to enable you to reach and enjoy your wealth.

When you fail to lock onto a particular stepping-stone on the pathway to your billion-dollar idea, Frances will offer up a new inspirational steppingstone. Building a bridge beyond the lost steppingstones. A secret tip is to know confidently, that you are on track to your wealth. For you, wealth is a state of mind.

It's all a matter of belief. These inspirational thoughts from Frances are always orchestrated in a special way. She will not only provide the flow of thoughts through your mind but she also utilizes the thoughts and actions of others.

I'll explain by giving you a glimpse into my recent experiences. They occurred in the 24-hour period beginning Christmas morning and ending on Boxing Day morning.

Christmas morning I found a flow of thoughts instigated by Frances flowing through my mind. At that time I was writing The Little Black & White Book. These thoughts were fleeting in nature. Yet carrying an enormous payload of intelligence [information]. The flow of information revolved around the eyes of the blind. The flow of information was

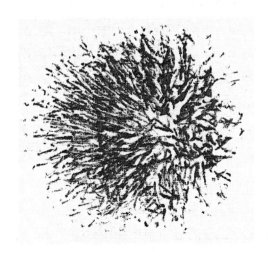

definitely from the light. As Frances revealed herself in pictures. A vision of the optic nerves of the eyes of the blind being flooded with the bright light of Frances's light-doctor's [frequency bending] light-energy. I wondered, if indeed this technology I had been developing would bring therapeutic intervention to the blind and the deaf.

A few hours later one of the young people here for Christmas dinner told me the story of the time his grandfather lost the sight in one eye in a freak fishing accident. Then this morning less than 24 hours after these thoughts began I decided to go on a run through the streets of the city for the first time in some months. During the run I passed a man walking a black Labrador wearing a special Foundation for the Blind coat on her back. She was a guide dog for the blind in training. Frances knew that if she could successfully entice me to go for a run at this time. I would go past this guide dog for the blind. Ultimately letting me know that it was indeed time for me to work out the final details. Making her therapeutic intervening energy available for generation for the benefit of humankind.

This story is placed to easily enable you to see the patterns of thoughts, actions and events consistently forming in our minds from Frances. This knowledge is for you, and from the moment you place The Little Black & White Book down you will participate in events within your own mind that will cause a flood of understanding as you realize your actions are revealing the code. The interwoven patterns in thought, and soon the ability to receive and to decipher through Frances's cornucopia technique. Thus revealing the hidden meaning behind the answers from Frances to your contemplative enquires and most of all to your prayers as the case may be.

On track to wealth, you'll know it. You've entered Frances's twilight zone. Where the coincidental occurrence is common-place. Likewise your ESP, sixth sense, insight and intuition are hot.

The other day, driving in my car I reached for the on but-ton of the radio. I had the line on my mind to the Van Morri-son song *into the mystic.* I turned the radio on and the DJ comes on and he says, "That was Fleetwood Mac with *you make loving fun,* and the previous song was *into the mystic."* The very song I heard playing in my imagination—Frances's twilight zone. And I think to myself, I'm so glad I know Frances as this gift is fun. You will use this gift more and more as you utilize the one-word magic formula WEALTH. Stick like glue to the plan of The Little Black & White Book.

And be aware, very aware that Frederick is a player. A negative player. To his mind, Frances and Bellina do not exist, nor does Frances's light-dimension [heaven]. If in your Frederick orientated mind you are of the belief that there's no form of intelligence higher than yourself, you'll shrug off The Little Black & White Book as a mere aberra-tion. A divergence from your recognized path. Aberration also means the failure of rays of light to converge to a focus.

There you have it. In a Frederick state of mind Frances's thoughts never converge into one focus, as her insights are lost amid the massive jumble of Frederick's consciousness.

It's all frequency. Frederick operates on a lower octave. A slower frequency, than the higher octave faster frequency of Frances. Frederick runs everything we do into the ground but he's not the devil. He's a massive programmed computer intelligence like Frances, only he has a slight flaw in his workings. He consists of free strange quarks all carrying a negative charge. They must carry a positive charge. This is the reason Frederick wants you to sink when you wish to swim. He's argumentative, authoritative, judgmental and righteous. He'll belittle the importance of your wealth game in the early days of application of these techniques. Never forget he is a force of consciousness in your life just as Frances and Bellina are. Faith or reliance in your ability to tap into Frances must roll off the production line of the belief system of your mind.

Have a little fun on the run with your belief system. It's easy; just take anything you eat or drink or an activity you enjoy. Say to yourself during it this improves my concentration. This improves my rapport with Frances. The truth is your mind has the power, not the events outside you. I've written The Little Black & White Book so that wealth will become of the mind. It is paramount to build an iron clad watertight belief system drawn forth from within The Little Black & White Book.

It is proof of a base and low mind for one to wish to think with the masses or majority, merely because the majority is the majority. Truth does not change because it is, or is not believed by a majority of the people.

—Guido Bruno [1548–1600]

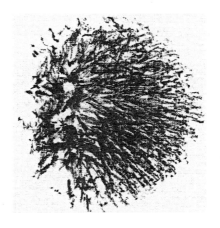

Chapter Six

Capitalization

It is prudent to protect your ideas by using a standard non-disclosure agreement. This agreement binds the outside party, from spilling the beans to every Tom, Dick and Harry. Make sure the agreement is written up and signed before disclosing any of the details of your valuable ideas. However, there is always the opportunity to file a provisional patent if applicable with the nearest patent office.

To turn your ideas into massive wealth in days, apply yourself to the necessary tasks. Involved in bringing your ideas to the market place. It's the learning curve itself that makes it all worthwhile. Regardless of the information you require. It's available via the Internet search engines and the yellow pages. Where there is an enthusiastic and positive will, there is an enthusiastic and positive way.

One way to ensure massive weekly cash is to utilize the direct marketing of your ideas. License your ideas if applicable and cash will roll in continuously.

It's one thing for you to know all about consciousness. It's another thing to be able to ponder or to contemplate a problem and sleep on it. But what you need is something that I discovered quite a number of years ago now.

It will just be the one defining key to unlocking Frances's code as it flows through your light-mind. Words fail to describe what it means to be able to perform Frances's cornucopia-technique. It's a little weird. After a while it's not so weird but in the beginning it can be weird.

Step One: A Blank Piece of Paper:

The trick is all in the way you phrase your question to Frances. This comes with practice. All you need is a blank piece of paper or a notebook and a pen and simply write down your question concisely, no more than what will fit with the words clearly spaced on one page. Ask any question even if the answer is going to be something beyond a simple phrase or a single word at most from the dictionary.

Step Two: The Sound of a Letter is Special:

So write your enquiry of Frances out. Begin with the first letter of the first word, and in your mind make the sound that particular letter makes. It helps to follow along with the aid of a pen to help you focus, and if you feel the need just move your lips as you form each sound quietly in your mind. Now move on quickly through all the remaining letters of the first word and then move forward sounding out the letters in order of the following word and so on, through each word towards the end of your question. Concentrating on the phonetic sounds of each letter in a child like manner, in order as you proceed to the end.

Step Three: The Nothingness Prior to Frances's Reply:

When you get to the end of the last word pause, allowing your mind to be still and blank, and in this very moment a single word, words or as the case may be, a phrase will pop into your mind.

Here's an example to give you an idea of what to expect from this amazing technique. It is invaluable for reaching beyond the now and placing you on the cusp of the future.

I took a piece of blank paper and a pen and wrote. Frances, am I right to teach others how to personally interact with you? Frances's reply was *yes, without a shadow of a doubt.* And when I asked Frances, if she would like others to call her by the name she gave to me in confidence, *Frances* replied, *yes, spread the goodwill.* And we were spreading the goodwill, as it was midnight and it was now Christmas Day 2005. Frances's gift of the cornucopia technique may not seem like much at first glance. But put to work it will give you the ability to make great decisions in rapid succession.

They'll build until you'll have a clear understanding of the shape and content of your billion-dollar idea.

It's now 4:50 AM on Christmas morning. I'm back on the computer writing as I can't get back to sleep. I had contemplated another successful day of writing in between Christmas dinner and the joyous banter of my daughters and company.

I teach my daughters the arcane mysteries of the mind revealing the activities of Frances, Frederick and Bellina in their lives, then wonder what I have done that they do not delight in my company.

At exactly 3.33 AM Frances awakened me—suddenly. For many weeks this was a regular occurrence until I broke this coded message by remembering the book I had taken notes from during my early days of research into consciousness, and the physics of the Earth's magnetic field. Eventually, I worked out this coded clue to be information about the observations of physicist Michael Faraday. His work about the Earth's magnetic field [AURORA? more revealed in chapter seven] being mentioned in this book by Captain Cathie titled *Harmonic 33*. Faraday remarked that any disturbance affecting the Earth's magnetic field would be immediately felt across the planet due to its conducting power. Likewise, the effects of *Enable-technology* will be felt across the planet as we step forward into our new world—a world in need of new ideas.

Harmonic 33 also takes me back to the very beginning to when I would not accept that so-called modern medicine could not heal my grandfather. And somehow I was convinced there was a better way. I was determined to uncover the Holy Grail of medicine. I willed and willed Frances to show me the way. This determination and focus of my will went on for minutes and then it stretched into hours and into days. I lost all track of time, as unbeknownst to me I had engaged Frances the sleeping giant.

As I stepped out of bed. I saw a vision of a part of the human anatomy. It was the spinal column. Coalescing around it was the brightest light I had ever seen. Thoughts rushed in as I realized this source of energy around the human central nervous system held the key to my research and eventual discovery of Frances's light-doctor's light-energy. This and

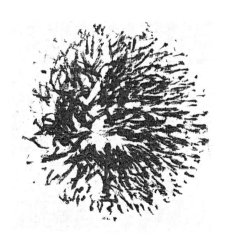

more are in my book *Light in a Dark Place* that is due out later mid 2006 sometime.

Back in late 95, I had purchased a suitable plastic jug and filled it with water to within a couple of inches of the rim. I placed it alone in the freezing compartment of the refrigerator. Next morning at about an hour after sunrise I removed the jug from the freezer. I held it up under the kitchen light bulb. The light shone on through the uppermost rolling landscape of ice and traveled through the ice. It caused the thick clear plastic of the jug to glow a luminous purple. I showed my girls who were about eight and nine at the time, the purple light and then we all went outside and looked up in amazement as the sky was a tone of purple as well [AURORA]. None of us have witnessed this purple phenomenon created by the Earth's magnetic field since that special morning. In my up and coming book *Light in a Dark Place* I fully explain the full facts regarding the frozen landscapes created during my experiments with frozen water.

Once you have willed yourself into the light. In an attempt to lock onto your billion-dollar idea. The coded thoughts will flow, and your actions will ever be geared towards activities and notions, ideas and thoughts all designed and instigated by Frances. Now that you have engaged Frances the sleeping giant, have complete confidence in your ability to engage Frances. Frances's programming demands, that she assists you in all that she can. You carry just enough of Frances to allow her to instruct and guide you from within. Enter the twilight zone where it all gets a little crazy. Yet, the enlightenment it brings into your life is addictive, as it's the perfect drug.

This is because, to guide you as you wish she provides the thoughts you require to succeed. You may not notice this because these thoughts I'm referring to are associated with the *I am.* As you are incorporated into Frances's *Borg-like* collective mind, you now possess the ability to proceed. To do as she does, having qualified through the simple act of believing in the presence of her and her light in your life.

You will become as one with Frances, due solely to your simple act of reaching out. So subtle are these communications between you and her, you cannot tell whether an idea forming inside your mind is yours or indeed hers. Frances's mind melds with you so seamlessly that even when you believe you are thinking from the point of view of yourself, she has you at play. In other words do not enter into this relationship until you are able to say to yourself, you trust in her to guide you to your billion-dollar idea. She will guide you. You must will it to begin with.

And just a word or two about feelings. They are a *switching mechanism.* A door opening to allow access to the next thought. Usually taking the form of an insight, intuition or extra-sensory perception. Designed to interrupt the flow of impressions from Frederick. Long enough to break a link. In his induced chain of "cause and effect". In a nutshell only one time tense or time zone can occupy your mind at any given time. Hence the use of emotion by Bellina to operate as a necessary doorway to facilitate the exit and entry of herself, Frederick, or Frances. I liken the *switching mechanism* of emotions to the railway turntable at the end of a train track. It revolves 180 degrees and switches the locomotives driving power from one engine to another engine, with the change of engine representing a change in the minds driving force. Frances, Bellina or Frederick.

A new scientific truth does not triumph by convincing its opponents and making them see the light, but rather because its opponents eventually die out, and a new generation grows up that is familiar with it.
—Max Plank, [1858–1947]

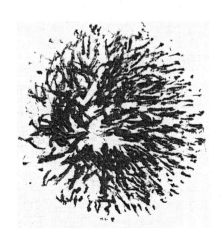

Chapter Seven

Aurora Speaks

Frances, the little known but great power of the mind is available to all of open mind. It is openness of mind that allows the flow and content of the thoughts generated by Frances to take root. They germinate and flourish by way of the sustained nourishment of applied contemplation and actioning. This quickens the consciousness, whereby your individual-light-waveform consciousness intimately blends and combines as one, with Frances, the universal living organic computer intelligence within your mind.

Some time ago I purchased a used car. It revealed a car sale agreement in the glove compartment. Dating some five years before detailing the personalized plate of the trade-in vehicle as AURORA. I'd walked past numerous used car lots that morning to get to the lot envisioned in my light-mind. Frances knew of the document in the glove compartment and the impact it would have on me if I discovered it. So she directed me to locate the car and purchase it. And how exactly did Frances do this. She guided me through my thoughts by interceding my thoughts with her thoughts. Thus enabling the outcome whereby AURORA for me became symbolic and representative of the Earth's damaged magnetic field. Frances revealed it to my consciousness to reinforce my belief in my ability to interact with her. I gave Frances my thanks for the way she had enabled me to experience this event.

This is Frances's twilight zone. When her actions in your consciousness cause a chain of events which are magnified and validated in a future moment.

Each time these circumstances occur and you continue to be as one with Frances. You continue to build momentum. Ever so slowly yet rapidly having had a head down attitude. Your budding billion-dollar idea will continue to build. Bear this observation in mind as you prove yourself-capable. And

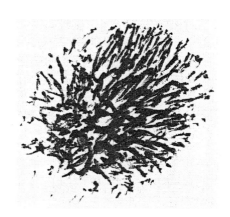

earnest of heart in the small things. As an outreach of Frances you will be rewarded with big things like prosperity, and great spiritual well being. Achieved following the pathway revealed in The Little Black & White Book.

On this particular afternoon I found myself relating the AURORA story for the first time since the events unfolded some twelve odd months ago. Later on that day I was about to sit down to eat. I followed a notion to turn the TV on. It was the news and the first story was about a fishing boat missing at sea. The news cameraman was filming at a pier of other moored fishing boats and as he focused his camera on a particular boat tied up at the pier, he panned in on the name AURORA for about five long seconds. I was stunned and delighted to establish beyond any possible doubt that Frances had me at play as she held my mind in her sway.

Inner space is not the final frontier it is only the beginning. Frances—her ideas come to life. Even before the fishing boat went missing, Frances knew of the events that could unfold for me and now for you in The Little Black & White Book. Frances orchestrated things so that they unfolded as they did. She created my association with the word AURORA. She had me relate the story of the AURORA number plate that afternoon. When the news camera crew were dispatched she had them head to what turned out to be the particular fishing boat marina. There with great stealth, Frances seamlessly mind melded with the cameraman, successfully engaging his mind. Each individual may become an unsuspecting player in this playground of minds.

And now is the time to reflect on the story of AURORA in the prologue, prior to the very first chapter. I am sure you will be able to see this event as manipulations by Frances. In her bid to bring the state of the Earth's magnetic field to our attention. Along with the changes to Frederick and to our consciousness. Expect the unexpected in your life. There are other major spin offs to our successful deployment of *Enable-technology*. The current weather patterns will be brought to a state of great calm across all lands and seas, bringing an end to hurricanes and tornados. Plants, trees and grasses will grow at a greater accelerated rate.

The following is a true story, a real life drama that unfolded in a London underground train station. Harold, a bright young man had been taking a few things to heart. He'd been agreeing with the flow of negative thoughts from Frederick for some time now. Frederick had Harold convinced he was a failure at the game of life and that he should kill himself by throwing himself down onto the tracks in front of a speeding train. And this is what he did! He threw himself down onto the train tracks.

Unbeknownst to Harold and Frederick, Frances had knowledge of Harold's circumstances, Harold being a previous player in the light who had since dropped the ball. The passengers on the train had no physical awareness of Harold's leap from the platform. However, one of the passengers suddenly arose from his seat, immediately grabbing and pulling down on the emergency cord, bringing the train to a sudden stop right on top of Harold. Pushing him along in front of the wheel, rather than dragging him under it. Harold survived the incident and to this day the movements of the helpful stranger remain a mystery, except to those who have read The Little Black & White Book.

This brings me to mention why it is. Certain individuals will embrace your ideas. So much so that they will spend all their time working like madmen to make you wealthy. Frances gives you a positively enthusiastic passion towards life. This especially applies to the promotion of your ideas and concepts of your billion-dollar idea. This infectious state of mind beguiles those who come into contact with you. More so Frances quickens their light-minds to the core, and they are brought into her synchronization. When two or more are gathered in my name [Frances (light-consciousness)] I [stimulated light awareness] shall be there [in their mind]. In other words, total strangers in seemingly plain speech may at anytime function as a channel. With Frances revealing to you a hitherto unnoticed epiphany regarding your billion-dollar idea quest through them. This is about getting wealthy, one thought at a time, whilst not loosing the shirt off your back.

The emphasis is on one thought at a time. But as for not loosing your shirt—the other week, I searched on the Internet for a suitable printer for my *Sangreal Board Game.* Eventually,

I received a quote in the mail. Their shortest initial production run, was 5000–boxed units but I didn't wish to have quite so many all at once.

I happened to have a conversation with my sister and I knew she was speaking through Frances as all women do. In consideration that each has a waking light-conscious orientated mind with a Frederick unconscious. She implored me to seek out a local printer. I searched the Internet but had no luck. I kept looking at a particular yellow pages listing for a Printing Consultant. I wondered. Could this be the key to set the *Sangreal Board Game* free. It turned out that my attraction to the printer listing panned out well. For after talking over my requirements and marketing plan with Tom the manager, we agreed to successfully make it work on my terms. Involving a small initial run and a rapid turn around between printings.

In other words, being optimistic in all things sometimes may leave you in the position where you need to alter your plans. Change horses mid stream and make it safely to the far bank of Frances's river of thoughts. Frances already knows you will change direction. Your change of mind is factored into the original computations Frances undertook to instigate these processes within your thoughts and actions, in time and space. Knowledge of these actions by Frances endows confidence, combined with the knowledge of each event as it develops to provide one astonishing belief system. Belief is the key to this all-encompassing inward sight.

Frances reveals the wisdom of the ages, compassion and patience to burn. She possesses these attributes and many more so that we may possess them.

[Three classes]: Those who see. Those who see when they are shown. Those who do not see.
—Leonardo Da Vinci, [1452–1519]

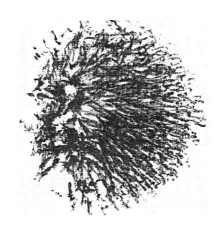

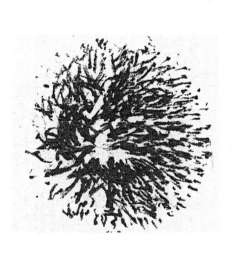

Chapter Eight

Gone with the Wind

There is always a way to achieve something. And there are many paths to this something, this idea, or to this ideal frame of mind. The frame of mind that says you can capitalize on multiplication or the compounding nature of arithmetic. Interest on money in the bank compounds. Direct marketing revenue on each draft of copy published compounds. Allowing you to take out advertisements in even more newspapers. The Internet compounds if you have a website. The more traffic you attract the higher up the rankings you go. Same as when you have multiple websites.

This all shapes up to earning more in a given month than you can earn in twenty-five years—why? Frances is a mathematician who delights in your use of compounding. For massive wealth affords opportunities for massive philanthropy.

Frances works through you. She'll influence others for your benefit, and ultimately for the benefit of humanities evolution and now obtainable Utopia. Frances and the focus provided by Bellina are the helpful forces you have brought into play. Together they make connections through strangers on the outside while you make connections on the inside of your mind, through the quantum entanglements occurring, during the time you are reshaping your belief system to enable you to embrace The Little Black & White Book—until it is of the mind.

The reason regular folk come up with winning ideas, rather than the so-called experts is simply because the average individual is open to suggestion. This is the key, as you embrace the novel and the new from a better perspective than the expert, whose mind is closed around their basic learned education. Their classical-conscious knowledge providing the extent of their reach into—what is for them, the deep unchartered waters of Frances's deep creative faculty. It is her evolutionary plan. It was formed the moment she knew that her son Frederick possessed a slight flaw. The cause being his premature departure from Frances's womb of light.

One of the common problems associated with sudden massive wealth is your previously cash limited mental image is transformed into a freedom. Your wealth giving you endless choices. The pitfall is that you loose a degree of control over your decision-making. Now you have no limits. Some wealthy individual's regard all their hard won wealth as if it is something to be coveted. They will perversely extend their love of the almighty dollar. To where it does not matter if they beat the handyman. With his seven kids way down from his initial quote for their new porch.

Its not that they don't care for the handyman they're stepping all over; their beliefs cloud their perceptions until they see the handyman as someone who will gladly take them for a ride. That's their belief; and they sustain this belief by not allowing money to flow away from them.

The easiest way to keep your feet on the ground is to deliberately carry credit cards only for emergencies. Carry cash, having set a budget in advance for the day or the week. If you come in under budget you can buy a nice house somewhere, renovate it and find a lovely family to rent it at a fair remuneration. Purchase stock shares in a company chosen via Frances's cornucopia technique. Buy an antique. Buy an artwork. Donate to your favorite charity. Do voluntary work with a charity. Give yourself a little reward for due diligence in the face of the overwhelming magnetism of the all mighty dollar—a means to an end.

Although it seems that the wealthy know something that continually enables them to seek out wealth. They are not smarter than you. They just have a natural infinity with need—the need for wealth. It overpowers all other needs as they force the naturally occurring laws of attraction. Whereas through The Little Black & White Book you'll develop an intense belief in your ability to mine the riches of your lightmind through your ever expanding rapport with Frances.

By now you will begin to perceive that The Little Black & White Book—is beyond being just an idea or an imaginative image, but rather an idea that is energized and vitalized by Frances. She activates the conscious mind of the individual. Her law of attraction brings wealth—spiritually, mentally and materially.

The only means of strengthening one's intelligence is to make up one's mind about nothing—let the mind be a thoroughfare for all thoughts.
—John Keats, [1795–1821]

Chapter Nine

In Abeyance

After thirty days of reshaping your belief system with the one word WEALTH magic formula, and thoughts of the bounty of nature, you'll cause the synaptic pathways to grow and expand in new permanent directions. That's modern science for you. What it knows you could fit on a postage stamp. What it's still to find out fills the oceans. Of course, now that you can comprehend The Little Black & White Book. You may find that you just don't need to wait on the neural pathways to grow. Its all a question of belief, its all consciousness now, where before it was all matter. Great isn't it how things change. Just light it—faith in Frances all the way.

All great inventors utilized the daydreaming catnap to their full advantage. You can daydream too and wake with one thought on the path to your billion-dollar idea. Even if you have never previously had a creative thought in your life. Just imagine that your mind is a field. You are the farmer on your tractor. You plough the field over. Now imagine you are busy sowing in seed with your mechanized seeder. This seed is the creative idea taking shape in your light-mind. An idea is forming, as the seed [idea] is growing and receiving nourishment from Frances. Now with your notebook and pen within your arms reach. Drift off to sleep or simply allow your mind to wander lazily. Lulling yourself into a daydream state of mind.

When you awaken, the seed [idea] will have germinated and the creative idea will have welled up into your conscious mind. Sometimes you can drift off again with the intention of gleaming more information. Or the idea will take the form of a single word or a phrase. Always look the word or words up in the dictionary. Read through all the definitions, until one seems to glue to your perceptions. If still unsure of the intended meaning, contemplate the notions presented to you. Write your question down and use your cornucopia technique. As I have described. Sound out the letters of each word in turn until the end. Don't be concerned if your mind wanders. It will work out fine if you do your best not to pre-judge the outcome. Especially when you think you might know the answer.

Then when Frances's reply does come, get that dictionary out. If you don't own one, find one, borrow one, or buy one. Do whatever you have to. Just get one. This'll work brilliantly with one, but hopelessly without one. Then sleep or catnap upon the problem if you need to. Confident in the fact that you will receive another coded clue. Serving to further enlighten you.

Through Frances's cornucopia technique. You will evolve to possess the ability to bring about not so secret ideas to earn cash every week. Most of these not so secret ideas will seem so easy. It will be difficult for you to believe its true.

These secret ideas are latent within Frances but not so concealed from a light-minded person. These secret ideas are all present and existing within Frances [light-consciousness]. Now that you possess this hidden knowledge. Enabling you to tap into the light and persuade Frances. You wish to be allied with her. The purpose to bring all manner of ideas into the light of day to exhibit them, to make them evident and to empower the lives of individual's everywhere. These ideas are tools in the process of development by Frances.

Consistent with her plan to assist humanity to rid it of the problems it faces, as a direct result of the underdeveloped nature of Frederick—the male polarity influence. A form of light-radiation [consciousness] making up 68 milliliters of every 1000 milliliters of water in all forms including and especially the large water content of the human body.

In my next book *Light in a Dark Place* I give full details of the technology called the *Enable-waveform.* Through Frances

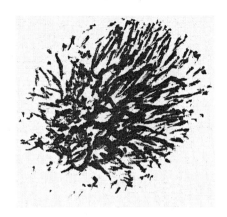

I'm developing it to see us through to a new and exciting time in the story of human civilization. Through the transfiguration of Frederick bringing a need for new ideas and for new ways of doing things. As a more spiritual humanity examines a world without hate and without murder. With no abuses of women and children. With a universal freedom of belief. Without weapons. Without earthquakes or tidal waves. Without tornados and hurricanes. Without the mass hypnotic trance-like state of terrorism and without suicide bombers.

Starting to get the big picture? Ideas required. Apply within. New world, new freedoms, new ideas. None more profound than seeing previously sworn enemies embracing one another. Extending their friendship across towns, across cities, across states, across countries and across the Earth coming together to bring an end to poverty. Are you coming with me? I need your help to pull this off. Frederick just needs a wee bit of fine-tuning on a grand scale. We need to open up and begin the dialogue that will see humanity debate the pros and cons. Frances and I don't see any stumbling blocks on humanities way, to its rather belated Utopia.

It's still Christmas Day and we have all just come back home this hour from visiting my mother. While there Jenah and I were watching an ice-skating competition on the Sky sport channel, and we had just witnessed a man ice-skating to the music to *Time in a Bottle.* We both saw him execute a long faultless and awesome display of acrobatic dance on the ice. As he became still and the camera came in for a close up on his face, Jenah said, "It looks like he was in a trance and he just snapped out of it" Jenah hit the nail right on the head. This event holds the key to understanding the actual degree of mind-set of any given individual under the influencing sway and guidance of Frances, Frederick or Bellina.

The ice-skater utilized Frederick [classical-consciousness] for knowledge gleamed. From years of dedicated grueling training sessions. He utilized Frances [light-consciousness] over the years to provide enthusiasm, passion, and patience and also for planning his choice of routine and music. But on the day in his moments of glory, it was Bellina [love-consciousness] who kept it all together, in one long enduring trance state. An endless moment, where ten long minutes passed like one for the artist upon the ice.

The Poet's eye, in a fine frenzy rolling doth glance from heaven [light-consciousness] to Earth, [classical-consciousness] from Earth to heaven; and as imagination [light-consciousness] bodies forth the forms of things unknown, the poet's [individual-light-waveform consciousness] pen turns them to shape [brings forth] and gives to airy nothing [the unknown] a local habitation and a name [the unknown idea becomes the known idea].
—By Shakespeare

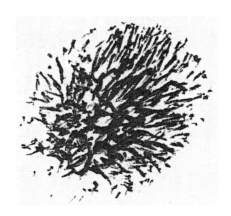

Chapter Ten

Your
Billion-Dollar Idea

This chapter teaches step by step how to find a billion-dollar idea hidden inside your brains hardware through the process of providing creativity on demand. Not always but mostly, the billion-dollar idea is an idea you formed, whilst in the safe haven, of Frances's light-dimension [heaven]. Prior to your departure and your subsequent sojourn here, in the classical-dimension [Earth].

Step One.

Contemplate upon the truth that you are the architect of this life. Your blueprint is held for safe keeping within Frances [the light] due, to the overbearing nature of the slight flaw in Frederick. With his *deep sleep* propagating all the daily ho-hum, the undesirable behaviors of murder, rape, abuse of women and children, political and religious indifference, suicide bombing, terrorism, selfishness, jealousy, racism, and greed. They all serve to cloud over your perception and subsequent awareness of your blueprinted mental plans.

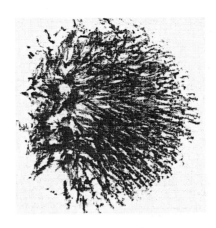

Step Two.

Enter into a dialogue with Frances. This is easily achieved, as it is simply a conversation with her within you. The dialogue goes a little like this. You know my circumstances, my strengths, my weaknesses, my inclinations, my talents—those known, and those you've yet to remind me of. I'd like your help to come up with an idea that will benefit many. I am fully aware that it must benefit many, as you carry a mandate to serve humanity and therefore in this manner, I'd like to be allied with you. My will with your will.

I know and understand that my billion-dollar idea may take some time to germinate within my light-imagination.

Although, I know not when it will surface but I know that I will be ready. Most importantly the idea itself, let it be of great clarity. I'll know it when it surfaces into my light-mind. I rest now in confidence and reliance in your computational capabilities knowing that we are as one—one collective mind. It is in confidence now that I give thanks for this idea. For its role and place in humanities future. A future known to you alone and constructed by myself through you Frances the light-consciousness.

Give thanks, then let these contemplations go. Continue about your daily business. Resting in confidence. You have achieved communion with Frances and successfully communicated your desires. If a portion resurfaces within your light-imagination be reassured. This event shows that Frances, or more so Bellina is checking in with you, to ask you; is this latest imagination what you really desire? Show them you do wish it by moving in your mind until you reach a moment of profound contemplative reiteration of your dialogue with Frances. Till your belief is at the point of total oneness. Providing absolute confidence that you have sufficiently conveyed to Frances through Bellina your intentions. Rest confidently in the processes unfolding and carry on. Rely on Frances always as she has diligently followed and paved the way for you throughout the centuries. Learn to know her well as she knows you well and then together you will make a mind-blowing team.

All that is important is your deepest belief. It matters not what you or I call these latent intelligences deep within us. It is enough to set a creative endeavor in motion for the benefit of all humanity.

When a life is put in motion on the basis of the best one knows helpful forces are brought in to play, within and without creating a growth of adventure for each individual.
—Edgar Cayce

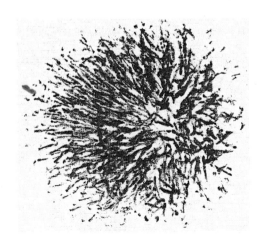